William H. Bird

The oriental miscellany

Beeing a collection of the most favourite airs of hindoostan, compiled and adapted

for the harpsichord

William H. Bird

The oriental miscellany
Beeing a collection of the most favourite airs of hindoostan, compiled and adapted for the harpsichord

ISBN/EAN: 9783742834287

Manufactured in Europe, USA, Canada, Australia, Japa

Cover: Foto ©Angelika Wolter / pixelio.de

Manufactured and distributed by brebook publishing software
(www.brebook.com)

William H. Bird

The oriental miscellany

THE
ORIENTAL MISCELLANY;

BEING A COLLECTION

OF THE MOST FAVOURITE

Airs of Hindoostan,

COMPILED AND ADAPTED FOR THE

Harpfichord, &c.

BY

William Hamilton Bird.

CALCUTTA

Print. By Jof. Cooper.

MDCCLXXXIX

To WARREN HASTINGS, Esquire,

SIR,

IF, like the generality of Dedicators, I ftudied the Name and Dignity only, of my Patron, I fhould be fully gratified in the great Refpectability of yours; but I have a higher Object in View, in the humble Hope, that the following Exertion of mufical Talents will prove acceptable; and that you will receive it as a Mark of the unfeigned Refpect, and invariable Attachment, with which I have the Honour to be,

SIR,

Your moft faithfully devoted,

Moft humble and

Obedient Servant,

CALCUTTA,
May 20th, 1789.

W. H. BIRD,

INTRODUCTION.

THE Compiler of the following airs heartily regrets the great infipidity which muft attend the frequent repetition of fubject, and their want of variety; and he fears the variations will but poorly compenfate.

He has ftrictly adhered to the original compofitions, though it has coft him great pains to bring them into any form as to TIME, which the mufic of Hindoftan is extremely deficient in. The airs of Cafhimere and Rohilcund are moft perfect and regular; but even thofe, on their being fung, need the grace of a Chanam*, and the expreffion of a Dillfook†, to render them pleafing.

The greateft imperfection, however, in the mufic in every part of India, is the total want of accompanyments; a third, or fifth, are addi-

---

* A famous Woman Singer.   † A male Singer, of great eminence.

tions,

tions, the Compiler, during a refidence of nineteen years in this country, and with the moft favorable opportunities, has never heard; and neither compofers or performers have had an idea exceeding an octave, though their modulations conftantly require relief to the ear.

The different ftyles of mufic in practice are,

Rekhtahs,

Teranas,

Tuppahs, and

Raagnies.

The Rekhtahs are moft admired, becaufe they are comprehenfible, and exceed all others in form and regularity.

The Teranas are performances of the Rohillahs, and fung only by men. They are next in perfection to the Rekhtahs, and have a great refemblance in ftyle.

The Tuppahs are wild, but pleafing, when underftood. They are of Mogul extraction, and have a peculiar ftyle of their own.

The

INTRODUCTION.

The Raagnies are fo void of meaning, and any degree of regularity, that it is impoffible to bring them into a form for performance, by any fingers but thofe of their country (Hindoftan); and they appear to be the efforts of men enraptured by words, to which they have added notes as their fancy and amorous flights have dictated.

The grand effentials in all mufic are, meaning, and expreffion; the Raagnies fometimes poffefs the latter, but are fo deficient in the former, that the Compiler has laid them afide. He has, however, felected one, as an example that will prove his folicitude to render the collection as complete as poffible; but, at the fame time evince, that to put a Raagnie into form, it will refemble, in too forcible a manner, a ftyle not its own.

The Sonata, at the conclufion, the Compiler claims as his own; though, to give it fome right to its prefent ftation, he has introduced a number of felect paffages from the airs. In the performance of them he earneftly recommends attention to the pianos, and fortes, as effentially neceffary. Some fongs of the ferodes (men-fingers) have a degree of MAESTOSO, which a good performer can eafily exprefs.

The

INTRODUCTION.

The fongs of Bengal are too lively to admit of much expreffion; and one, or more, may be danced to as cotillions; the Minores have been added, for that purpofe.

This being the firft public mufical attempt of the Compiler's, he hopes for indulgence from his judges. And though the performance fails in perfection, that they believe his humble endeavours have been anxioufly exerted for the entertainment of his friends, and the publick.

LIST OF SUBSCRIBERS.

A.

ANDERSON, Mifs, - - 1
Adair, Robert, Efq. - - - 1
Amherft, W. K. Efq. - - - 2
Arnold, Lieut. - - - - 1
Alcock, Lieut. - - - 1
Afhworth, Lieut. - - - 1
Auriol, J. Efq. - - - - - 1
Allen, C. Efq. - - - - 1
Apfley, Capt. - - - - 1

B.

BRISTOW, Mrs. - - - 1
Barlow, Mrs. - - - - - 1
Burrington, Mifs, - - - - 1
Burgh, Mrs. - - - - 1
Birch, Mrs. - - - - - 1
Bruce, Mrs. - - - - - 3
Brightman, Mifs, - - - - 1
Burrington, Col. - - - 1
Brooke, W. A. Efq. - - - 2
Bird, S. Efq. - - - 3
Barlow, G. H. Efq. - - - 1
Bathurft, R. Efq. - - - 2
Blunt, Sir Charles, Bart. - - - 1
Bateman, Major, - - - 1
Bruce, Capt. Rob. - - - 1
Brown, Mrs. Anne, - - - 1
Baillie, James, Efq. - - - 1
Hoyd, George, Efq. - - - 1
Boyd, William, Efq. - - - 1

COPIES

Barber, C. Efq. - - - 1
Browne, Lt. G. S. - - - 1
Baillie, Lieut. L. - - - - 1
Bellas, Enfign J. H. - - - 1
Bird, Enfign J. J. - - - 1
Baillie, W. Efq. - - - 1
Benfon, Lieut, - - - - 1
Burges, Y. Efq. - - - - 1
Boujannier, Capt. - - - - 2
Bridgewater, Enfign R. P. - - - 1
Bruce, R. Efq. - - - - 1
Biddulph, —Efq. - - - - 1
Bagfhaw, Lieut. R. M. - - - 1
Brooke, T. Efq. - - - - - 5
Bird, Lieut. H. F. - - - - 1

C.

CORNWALLIS, Earl, 1
Cox, Mrs. S. - - - - - 2
Cockerell, Mrs. - - - 1
Calvert, Mrs. - - 2
Cockerell, Colonel, - - - - 1
Cullen, Capt. J. P. - - - 1
Campbell, Capt. J. - - - 1
Cameron, Capt. W. N. - - - 1
Cuft, Capt. T. - - - 1
Cox, Capt. S. - - - - - 1
Cunningham, Capt. D. - - - 1
Cochrane, James, Efq. - - - 1
Crockatt, Lieut. - - - 1
Collins, Capt. - - - - - 1
Campbell, Archibald, Efq. - - 2

copies.

Cuming, Enfign, - - - - - 1
Crifp, B Efq. - - - - - - 1
Cockerell, C. Efq. - - - 1
Chimpain, J. Efq. - - - - 1
Crifp, J. Efq. Governor of Bencoolen, 1
Clark, Major, - - - 1
Cumming, W. Efq. - - - 1
Cock, Mr. V. - - - 2
Collins, Efq. - - 1
Chatfield, Major, - - - 1

D.

DOUGLASS, Mrs. - - - - 1
Dent, Mrs. - - - - 1
Duff, Col. - - - - 1
Duncan, Major, - - - - 1
Dalrymple, Capt. - - - - 1
De Caftro, Capt. - - - - 1
Don, Lieut. P. - - - - 1
Davies, Lieut. Robt. - - - 1
Tandidge, G. Efq. - - - 1
Delamaine, Lt. J. - - - - 1
Dyer, Major, - - - - 1
Dickfon, Capt. A. R. - - - 1
Davidion, Lieut. - - - - 1
Devis, Mr. William, - - - 2

E.

EVANS, Mrs. - - - 1
Erfkine, Colonel, - - 1
Eyres, Colonel, - - - 1
Evans, Lieut. S. - - 1
Edwards, Lieut. - - - - 1

F.

FORBES, Mrs. - - - 1
Farquharfon, Mifs, - - - 2
Frith, Mrs. - - - 1
Forbes, Lieut. Col. - - - 1
Farmer, Major, - - - - 1

copies.

Frith, Captain, - - - - 1
Fawcett, Captain, - - - 1
Frazer, Lieut. C. - - - - 1
Frith, Lieut R. - - - - 1
Fenwick, E. Efq. - - - - 1
Fleming, J. Efq. - - - - 1
Farquharfon, J. Efq. - - - 1

G.

Greene, Mrs. - - - - 1
Grant, Mrs. R. - - - - 2
Gafcoigne, Mrs. - - - 1
Greene, Major, - - - - 1
Grant, R. Efq. - - - 1
Grand, G. F. Efq. - - - - 2
Grant, Capt. L. - - - 1
Grace, Capt. H. - - - 1
Gahan, Lieut. R. - - - 1
Grant, G. F. Efq. - - - 1
Green, Lieut. - - - - 1
Gardiner, Capt. - - - - 1
Gordon, Lieut. John. - - 1
Gladwin, F. Efq. - - 1
Graham, J. Efq. - - - 1
Golding, Lieut. - - - - 1
Gafcoigne, Lieut. - - 1
Grant, J. Efq. - - - 3
Grant, C. Efq. - - - 2
Graham, J. Jun. Efq. - - 1
Gardiner, J. P. Efq. - - 1
Goodlad, R. Efq. - - - 2
Gofling, R. Efq. - - - 1

H.

HASTINGS, Mrs. - - - - 1
Hay, Mrs. E. - - - 1
Haftings, W. Efq. - - - 2
Hyndman, Capt. H. - - 1
Hay, Major, - - - - 1
Hamilton, Capt. R. - - - 1

	COPIES.
Helme, Mifs, - - - - -	2
Hay; Major, - - - - -	1
Hamilton, Capt. R. - - -	1
Haynes, Capt. J. - - - -	1
Heffernan, Lieut. M. - - - -	1
Hardy, Major, - - - - -	1
Hall, Phineas, Efq. - - - -	1
Hardwick, Thomas, Efq. - -	1
Hamilton, G. Efq. - - - -	1
Harvey, H. Efq. - - - -	1
Haldane, J. Efq. - - - -	1
Hartley, B. Efq. - - - -	1
Hickey, W. Efq. - - - -	1
Hyde, J. Efq. - - - - -	1

I. J.

IVES, Mrs. - - - - -	1
Johnfon, R. Efq. - - - -	1

K.

KIRKPATRICK, Mrs. - - -	1
Kerr, Mifs Eliza, - - - -	1
Kyd, Col. - - - - - -	1
Kyd, Capt. - - - - -	2
Knowles, Capt. - - - -	1
Keighly, J. J. Efq. - - -	1
Keating, C. Efq. - - - -	1
Keafbury, Lieut. - - - -	1
Kennaway, R. Efq. - - - -	2

L.

LARKINS, W. Efq. - - -	1
Law, T. Efq. - - - -	1
Laird, J. Efq. - - - -	1
Lumfden, Lieut. D. - - -	1
Long, Lieut. T. - - - -	1

M.

MURRAY, Mrs. P. - - -	1
Mackenzie, Mrs. - - - -	2

	COPIES.
McLeod, Mrs. Col. - - - -	1
Maule, Mrs. - - - -	1
Murray, Mr. J. - - - -	1
McKenzie, Major, - - - -	1
Murray, Lieut. Col. P. - -	2
Melville, J. Efq. - - - -	1
Maxwell, Captain, - - - -	2
MacDougall, Captain, - - -	1
Morris, Capt. J. - - - -	1
Montague, Capt. E. - - - -	1
Macan, Capt. J. - - - -	1
Macleod, G. Efq. - - -	1
M'Cullock, F. Efq. - - -	1
Mouggach, Lieut. - - - -	1
M'Corkill, Lieut. J. - - -	1
Mence, Major, - - - - -	1
Mafon, B. Efq. - - - -	1
Montgomery, A. Efq. - - -	1
Mordaunt, Capt. H. - - -	1
Munro, W. R. Efq. - - -	1
Miller, John, Efq. - - - -	1
Middleton, Lt. Col. - - -	1
Middleton, Enf. G. - - -	1
M'Kenzie, Capt. - - - -	1
M'Dougall, Efq. D. H. - -	1
Mee, Benjamin, Efq. - - -	1
Mercer, Laurence, Efq. - -	1
Maxwell, Lieut. James, - -	1
Morrifon, Lieut. A. - - -	1
Middleton, S. Efq. - - -	1
Moore, Wm. Efq. - - - -	1

N.

NICHOLLS, Mrs. - - - -	1

O.

OCHTERLONY, Lieut. D. - -	1
Orr, J. Efq. - - - -	1
Oldfield, C. Efq. - - - -	1

	copies.
O'Halloran, Lieut. J. - - -	1
Oehme, Mr. - - - -	1

P.

Plowden, Mrs. - - - -	1
Polhill, Mrs. - - - - -	1
Peacock, Mifs, - - - -	1
Palmer, Major, - - - -	2
Pringle, Capt. J. - - - -	1
Pringle, Capt. A. - - - -	1
Playdell, J. M. Efq. - - -	1
Pigott, Lieut. T. P. - - -	1
Palmer, Lieut. W. G. - - -	1
Perreau, Montague, Efq. - - -	1
Pearce, ——, Efq. - - - -	1
Pierard, F. Efq. - - - -	1
Price, Mr. J. Jun. - - - -	1
Palmer, Lieut. S. - - - -	1
Pote, E. Efq. - - - - -	1
Power, Mr. T. - - - -	1

R.

RAMSAY, Mrs. - - -	1
Rous, C. W. B. Efq. - - -	2
Rawftorne, Lieut. Col. - - -	1
Ruffell, Major, - - - -	1
Rayne, Capt. R. - - - -	1
Radcliffe, C. Efq. - - - -	8
Ranken, Lieut. W. - - -	1
Redford, Mr. - - - -	1
Robertfon, Col. - - - -	1
Roberts, C. Efq. - - -	1

S.

SMITH, Mifs - - - -	1
Stuart, Hon. C. - - -	1
Shore, J. Efq. - - - - -	1
Scawen, J. Efq. - - -	1
Skelly, Major, - - -	1
Stuart, Col. R. - - -	1

	copies.
Sandford, Capt. E. - - -	1
Short T. V. Efq. - - -	1
Stuart, Senr. Lieut. C. - - -	1
Sandys, Lieut. W. - - -	1
Stewart, Lieut. W. - - -	1
Shuldham, Lieut. J. - - -	1
Staunton, Lieut. T. - - -	1
Scrimgeour, Capt. - - -	1
Speke, P. Efq. - - - - -	1
Swainton, W. Efq. - - -	1
Scott, Lieut. S. - - - -	1
Shaw, Lieut. - - - - -	1
Scott, Capt. D. - - - -	1
Spottefwood, W. Efq. - - -	1

T.

TOMLINSON, Mrs. - - -	1
Taylor, M. S. Efq. - - -	2
Tiffeah, J. Efq. - - - -	1

V. U.

VIBART, Captain, - - -	1
Upjohn, Mr. A. - - - -	1

W.

WOODBURN, Mrs. - -	1
Williams, Mifs, - - - -	1
Ware, Col. Chas. - - -	1
Woodburn, Major, - - -	1
Wilfon, Capt. G. - - -	1
Williamfon, Capt. S. - - -	1
Wood, Capt. J. - - - -	1
White, Lieut. H. V. - - -	1
Wroughton, W. Efq. - - -	1
Watherftone, Lieut. R. - - -	1
Wroughton, Lieut. - - -	1

Y.

YEATS, Mr. T. - - -	1

THE GUT.

Variation 2d

Variation 3d.

R E K H T A H.

Sakia! fuful beharuſt,

Chanam,

Andante

Volti preſto

T U P P A H.

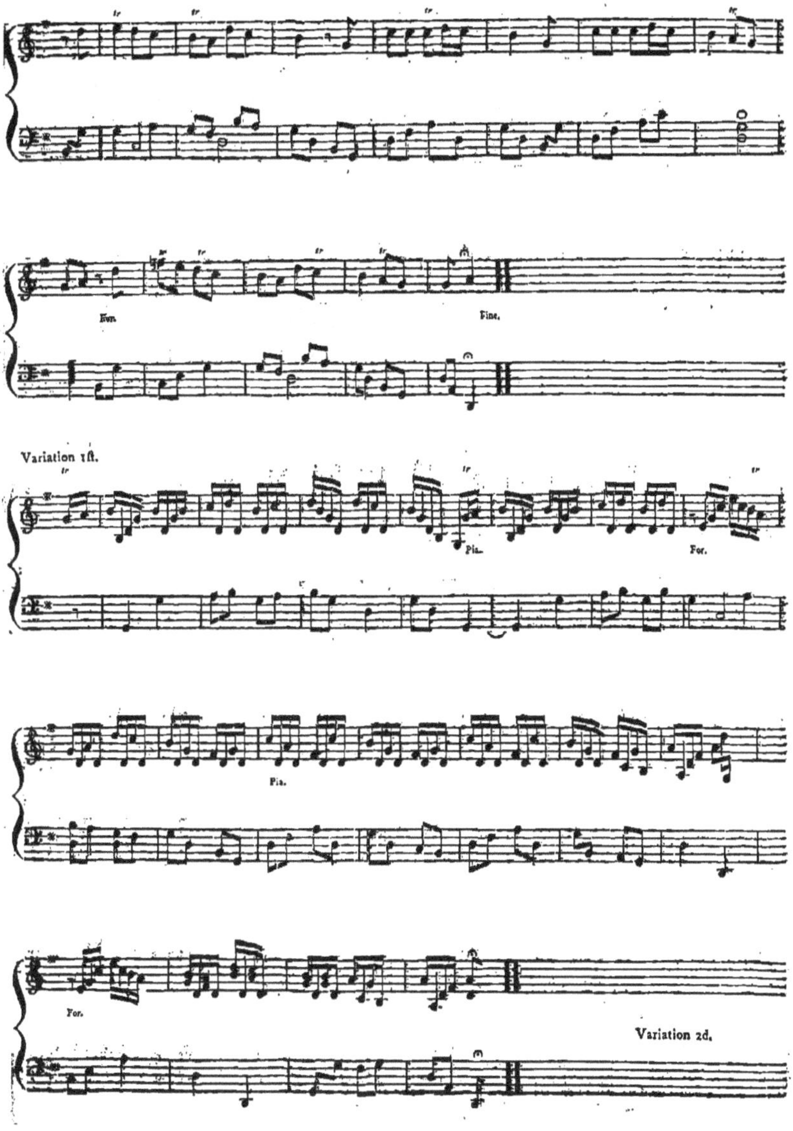
For.
Fine.
Variation 1ſt.
Pia.
For.
Pia.
For.
Variation 2d.

Variation 2d.

Variation 3d.

Da Capo.

R E K H T A H.

رخته

Mutru be khoofh nuwa bego —   Chanam.

Andante.

TUPPAH.

Ouwul keh mura buh iſht razee kurdee.

Dillfook.

Variation 2d.

Pia.

Pia.

Pia.

For.

Da Capo.

R E K H T A H.

Soonre mashookan! be wufa!

Chanam.

Amorofo.

Voli prefte

Variation 1st.

Poco Allegro.

Da Capo.

Cadenza.

Variation 2d.

Variation 3d.

Cadenza.

For.

Pia.

Cadenza.   D. C.

REKHTAH.

رکهته

Hy bashud, o hy bashud,   Chanani.

Vivace.

Pia.
Adagio.   Vivace.

Pia.
Adagio.   Vivace.   Pia.

Fine.

TUPPÀH

Ai purri chehreh !

Dillfook.

Affetuofo.

Fine.   Pia.   For.   Pia   Da Capo.   For.   D. C.

Variation.

Poco Andante.

Pia.   For.   Pia.   For.

Pia.   For.   Pia.   Forte.   D. C.

T E R A N A.

نرانا

Aute ſe bole, bundoo !

Serodes,

REKHTAH.

Gid a Shumba,

Bengal.

Vivace.

Pia.

For.

Fine.

Variation 1st.

Volti preſto

Variation 2d.

Variation 3d.

D. C.

REKHTAH.

TUPPAH.

Dande ka la,   Dillfook.

Variation 2d.

Volti presto

T E R A N A.

Forte

Pia.   For.

:St.

:St.

Toom co fumſhouta,   **T U P P A H.**   Dillſook.

Adagio.

Pia.   For.

Volti preſto

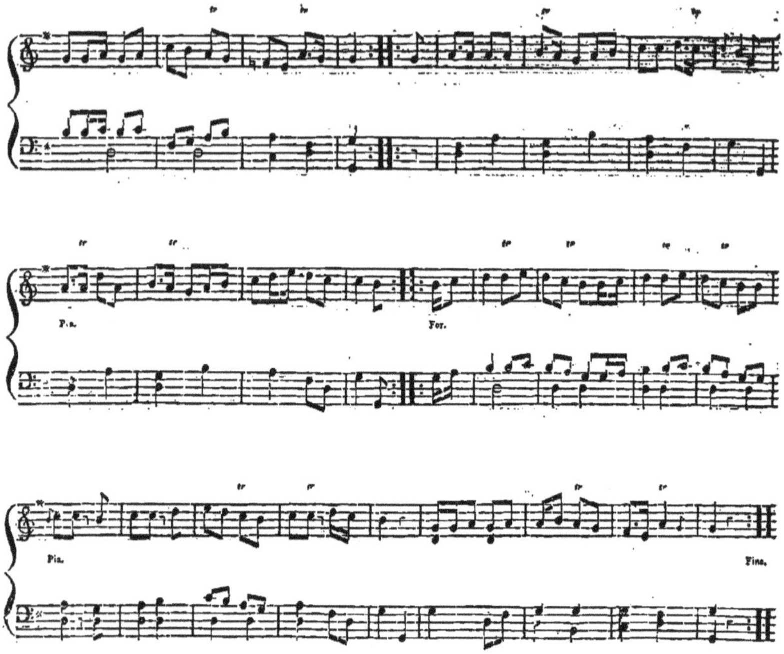

R E K H T A H.

Mera peeari ab,ia re

Ruttea

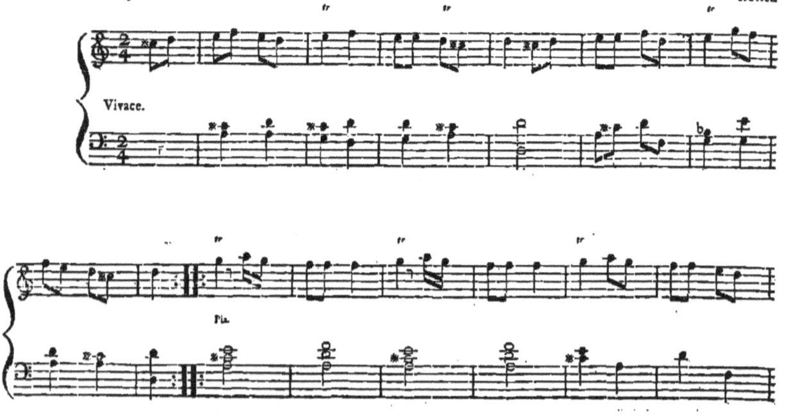

Variation 1st.

Volti presto

Variation 2d.

Kanja kia,   Dillfook.

Affetuofo.   Pia.

Pia.   Fina.

Variation

D. C.

R

Volti preſto

R E K H T A H.

Quoee fera que futke,

Serodes.

Andante.

Piu.

Fine.

R E K H T A H.

Shifch bur fhrob,

Bengal.

Vivace.

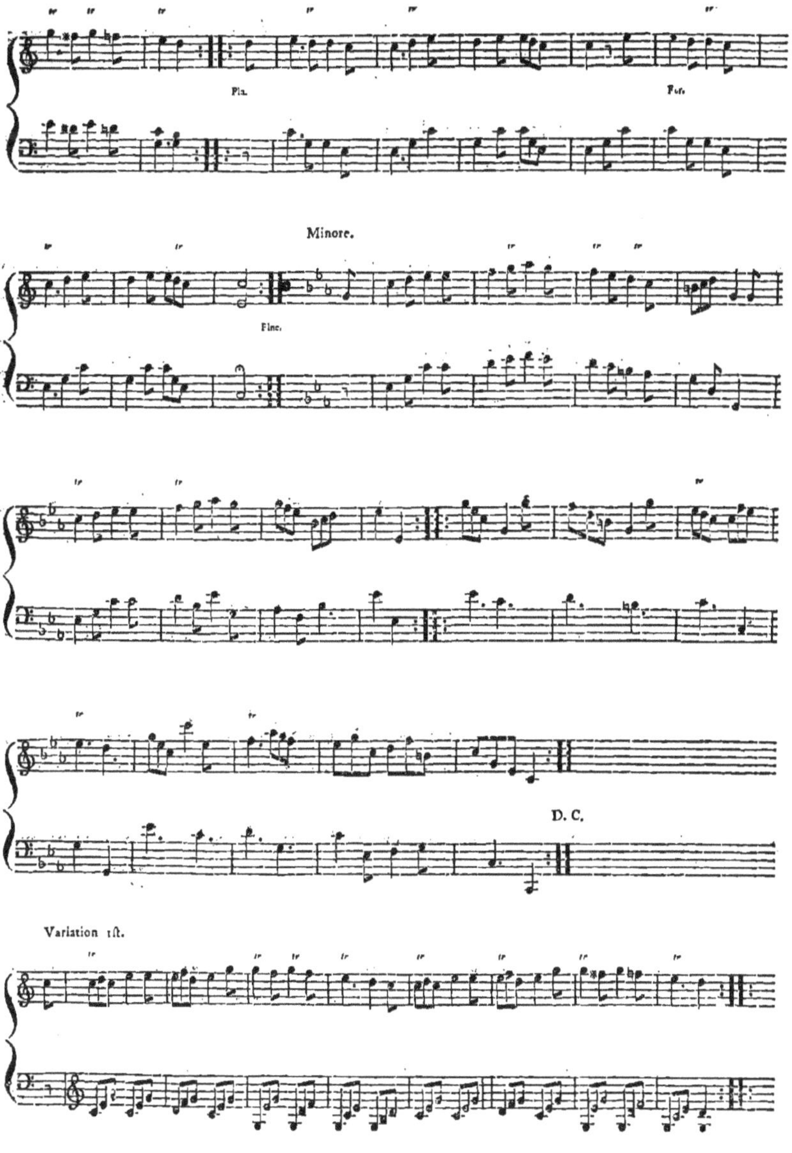
Pia.
For.
Minore.
Fine.
D. C.
Variation 1st.

Variation 2d.

T E R A N A.

Ya laum, ya laum,

Serodes.

Adagio,

Fine.

Fortif.°.   D. C.

RĖKHTAH.

Dill ne danne leeá re,   Patan:

Andante.

Pia.

For.   Fine.

Variation 1st.

Pia.   For.

Piu Andante.

Variation 2d.

Variation 3d.

D. C.

TUPPAH.

REKHTAH.

Hi bibbi mon karella,

Bengal.

Vivace.

Pia.

Pia.

For.

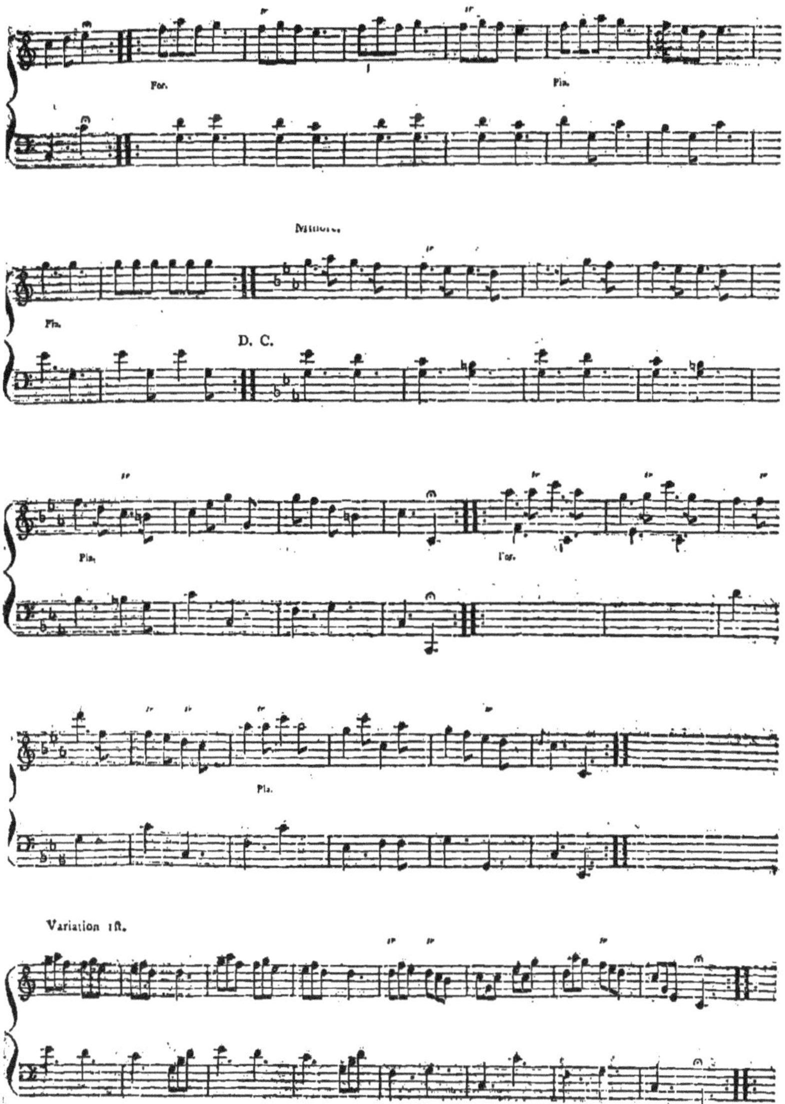
For.
Pia.
Minore.
Pia.
D. C.
Pia.
For.
Pia.
Variation 1st.

D. C.

Variation 2d.

Variation 3d.

Poco Adagio.

Pia.   Piaᵒ.

Pia.   For.

D. C.

O I yaar O I   Patan.

Affetuofo.

Pia.

For.

Pia.   Fine.

Pia.
Largo.

REKHTAH.

TUPPAH.

Piar mera soon, — Patan.

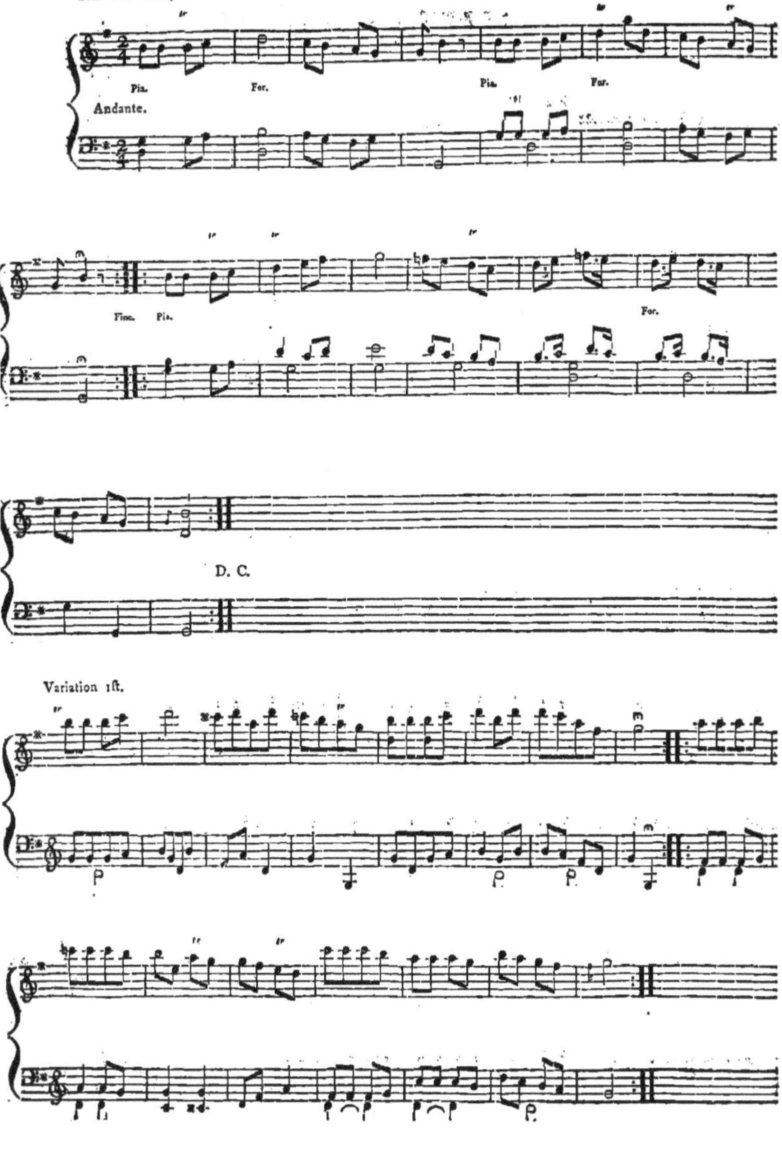

38

Variation 2d.

Variation 3d.

A la Kanoon *.

Variation 4th.

Presto.

* A Dulcimer.

R A A G N E Y.

R E K H T A H.

Bengal. (Dandies.)

Vivace.

Pia.

For.

Fine.

Variation 1st.

Variation 2d.

Variation 3d.

Pia.   For.

Pia.   For.

R E K H T A H.

Munni bibbi nocharee,

Andante.

Pia.

Fot.

Fine.

REKHTAH.

44

Variation 2d.

Minore.

F I N I S.

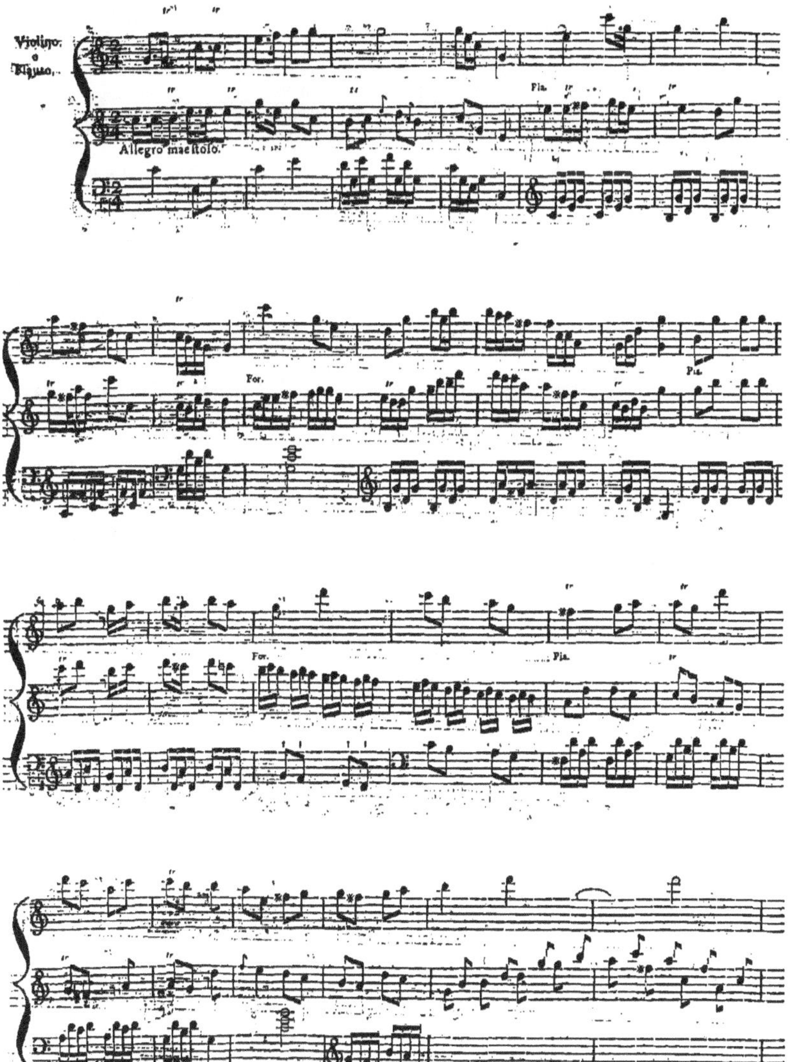

Volti presto

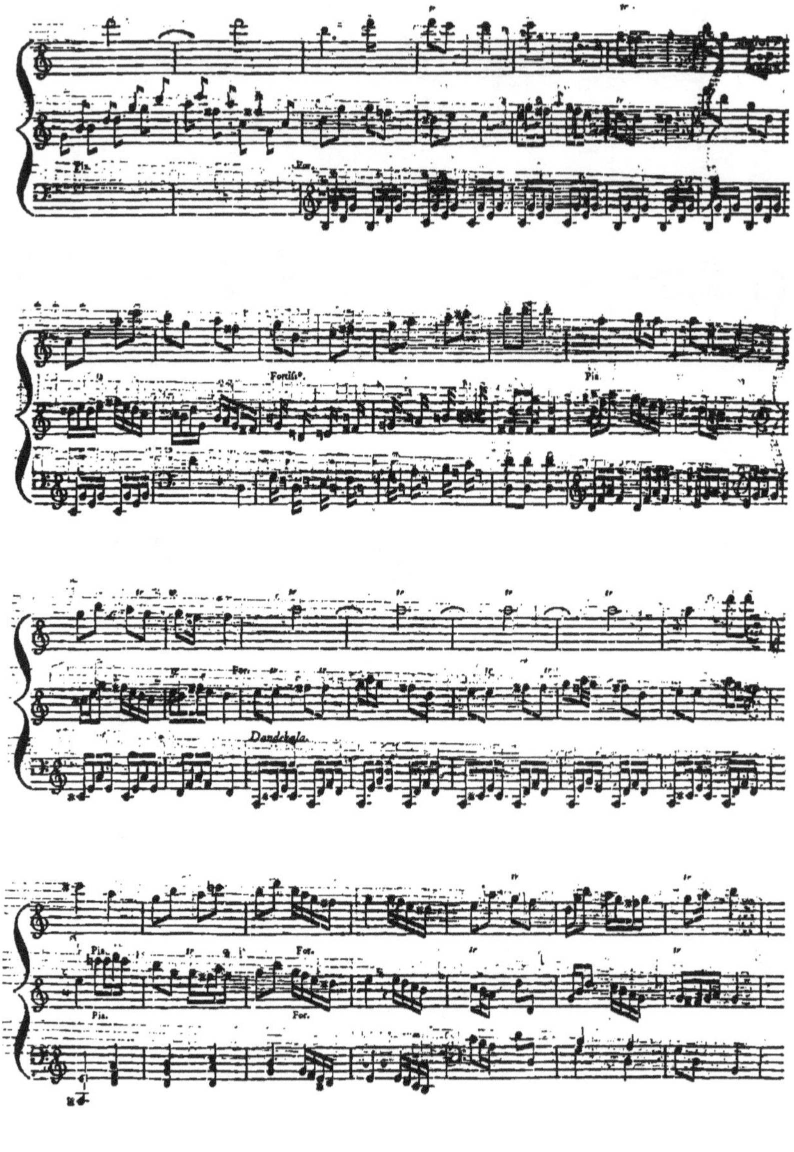
Pia.
For.
Fortiss°.
Pia.
For.
Pia.
For.
Pia.
For.

bhisha mera bia.

Hi puree chera.

Volti presto.

Ai mera piaree!

Ya Laum.

Volti preſto.

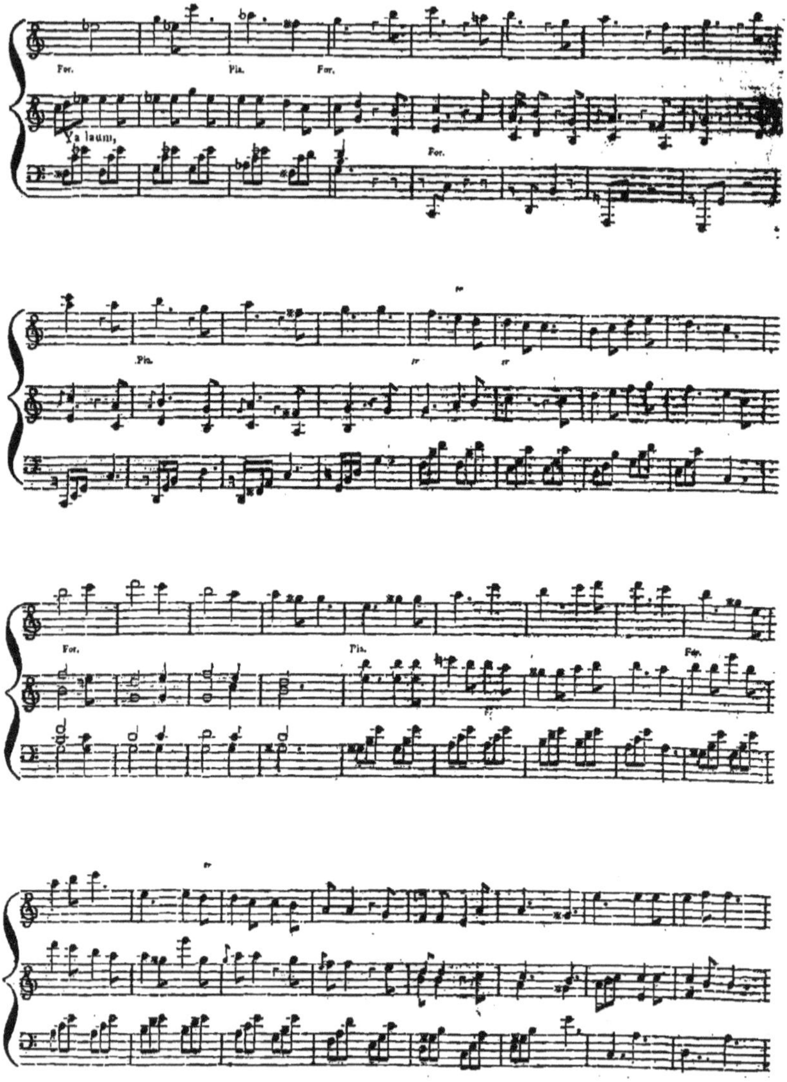
For.
Pia.
For.
Ya laum,
For.
Pia.
For.
Pia.

MINUETTÓ.

Gid a fhumba,

J I G G.

Shifch bur throb,

For.

Pia.

Volti preftiffimo.

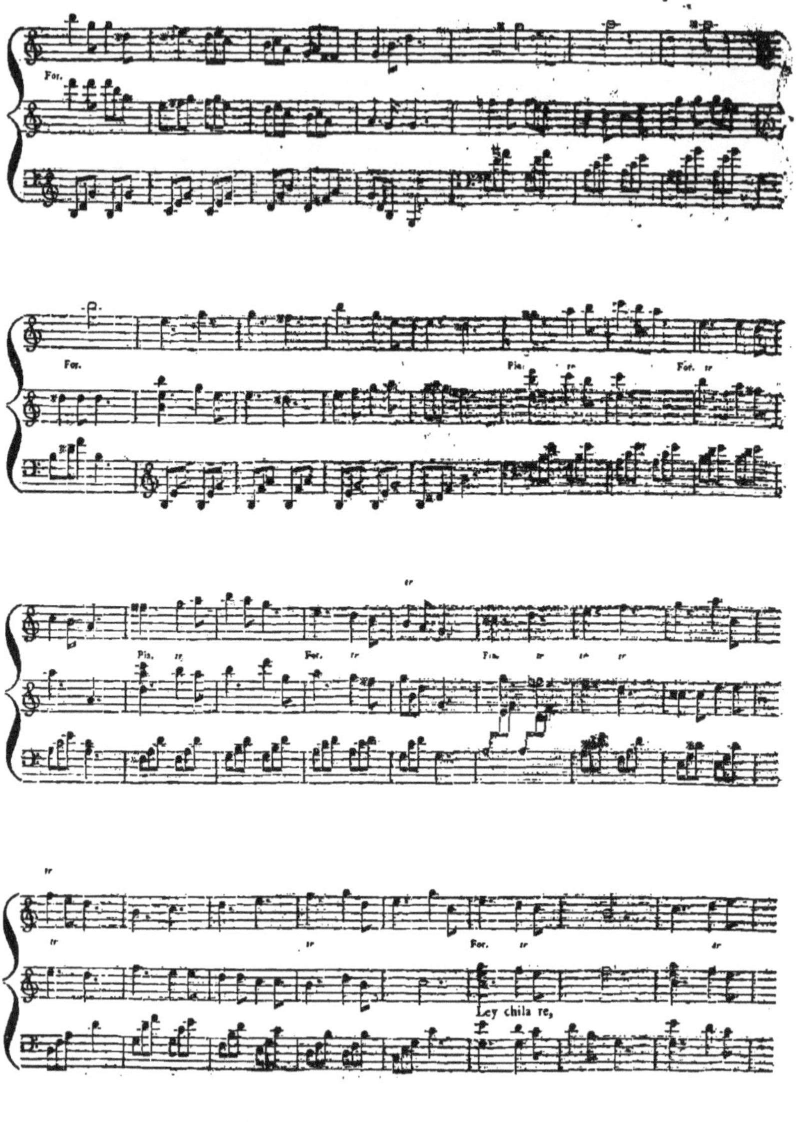
For.
For.
Pia.
For.
Pia.
For.
Pia.
For.
Ley chila re,

Fine.

For the Guitar.

SYMPHONY.

Allegro.

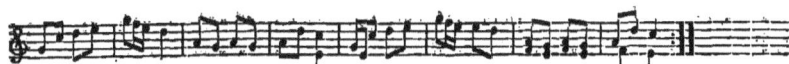

Variation 1st.

Variation 2d.

Sakia! fuful baharust.

Andante.

D. C.

Volti presto.

Da Capo.

Kia kam keea dil ne?

Largo.

Variation.

Mutru be khoofh nuwa bego,

Andante.

Ouwul keh mura buh ifht razee kurdee,

Andante.

Da Capo.

Variation 1ft.

Variation 2d.

Da Capo.

Soonre maſhukan! be wuſa!

Amoroſo.

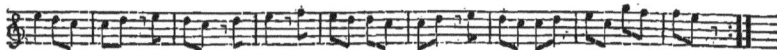

Variation.

Hy baſhud, O hy baſhud!

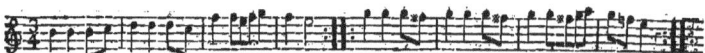

Con ſpirito.

Adagio.

Hi purri chehreh!

Affetuoſo.　　　　　　　F.　　　P.　　　P.　　　Fine.

P.　　　　　F.　Da Capo.　　　　　F.　Da Capo.

Variation.

Poco Andante. P.　　　　　F.　　　　　P.　　　　　F.

P.　　　　　F.　　　　P.　　　　　　Da Capo.

Aute fe bole bundoo !

Andante.

Adagio. P.

Allegro. F.　　　　　　Fortifs.

Gid a fhumba,

Con fpirito.

F.　　　　　　　　　　　　Fine.

Variation.

Shusha myra bear,

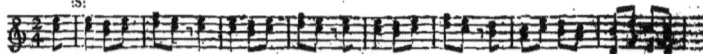

Adagio.

Da Capo.

Dandee kala,

Affetuofo.

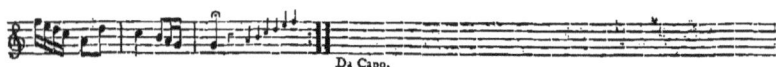

Da Capo.

Variation.

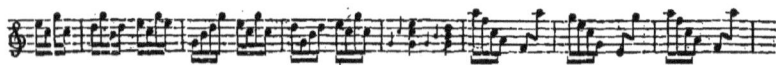

Dandera vakee,

Con Spirito.

Toom ko fum fhouts,

Adagio.

Mera peeari ab ia re,

Vivace,

Fine.

Variation.

Kan ja kia,

Affetuofo.

Da Capo.

Quoee fera que futkeh,

Andante.

Fine.

Shifch bur fhrob,

Con fpirito.

Minore.

Da Capo.

Variation.

Ya laum, ya laum,

Adagio.

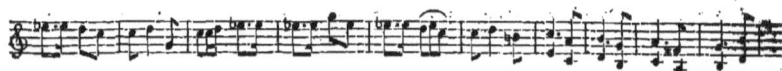

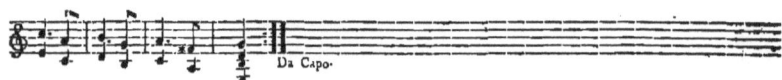

Da Capo.

Dil ne danne leea re,

Andante.

Variation 1st.

Fine.

Variation 2d.

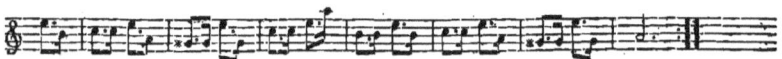

Variation. 3d.

Da Capo.

Mera mutchelli!

Allegro.

:S:

Fine,

:S:

:S:

Deem tere ha,

Andante.

Volti presto.

Hi bibbi mon karella,

Allegro.

Da Capo.

Variation.

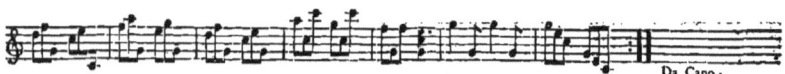

Da Capo.

O yaar oh !

Andante.

Fine. Adagio.

Da Capo.

Ley chila re,

Con spirito.

Fine.

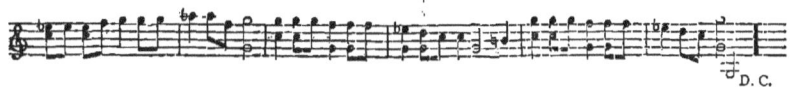

D. C.

Piar mera foon,

Andante.

Da Capo.

Variation 1st.

Variation 2d.

Rekhtah.   Dudleu

Allegro.

Variation.   Fine.

Mooni bibbi nochare,

Andante.

Rewannah kifly,

Andante.

The End.